Spectacular Schools

Paul Cookson and **David Harmer** spend most of their time writing poems and performing them. They are always spectacular in schools, whether performing separately or together as *Spill The Beans*.

They would both like to go to a spectacular school for electric-guitar-playing, five-a-side-footballing, fast-bowling, six-hitting, sweet-eating cricketers.

Paul and David are married, but not to each other. Paul lives in Retford with Sally, Sam and Daisy. David lives in Doncaster with Paula, Lizzie and Harriet.

Yvonne Chambers and **Maxwell Dorsey** share a studio near the Arsenal ground, with Sue, and Arnie the dog.

Other books from Macmillan

SPILL THE BEANS

Poems by Paul Cookson and David Harmer

WHO RULES THE SCHOOL?

Poems chosen by Paul Cookson

WHO RULES THE SCHOOL NOW?

Poems chosen by Paul Cookson

Spectacular Schools

poems chosen by

Paul Cookson and David Harmer

Illustrated by
Chambers and Dorsey

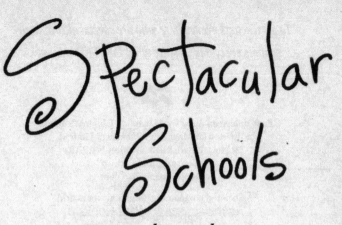

MACMILLAN CHILDREN'S BOOKS

To all teachers everywhere who are spectacular in their
schools every day, despite what OFSTED may say.

First published 2004 by Macmillan Children's Books
a division of Macmillan Publishers Limited
20 New Wharf Road, London N1 9RR
Basingstoke and Oxford
www.panmacmillan.com

Associated companies throughout the world

ISBN 0 330 39992 6

3 5 7 9 8 6 4 2

A CIP catalogue record for this book is available from
the British Library.

Printed and bound in Great Britain by Mackays of Chatham plc, Kent

'Higher Education' by Stewart Henderson, from *All Things Weird and Wonderful*
by Stewart Henderson (2003), Lion Books

Contents

Circus School Reception Class

My little brother Adam
has started circus school

He can't do the trapeze or the tightrope
until he's six.

He's scared of horses and he can't eat fire
because it makes him burp.

He's learning to juggle two teddy bears
and to throw rubber knives at a wooden
    man.

For homework he balanced
Mum and Grandma on his head.

They were quite impressed, told the teacher
'Not bad for a five year old.'

In PE he wears a leopard-skin vest
and baggy shorts.

He pulls a car full of clowns across the ring
with a skipping rope round his toe.

Then rips up a telephone directory
and sucks his thumb.

Then he has his milk and a biscuit
goes home for a sleep.

Next year he's in Year One
doing lion taming.

Right now he's in the sandpit
learning how to walk on stilts.

David Harmer

WANTED ALIVE:
New Teacher for Cowboy School

Are you a sharpshooter
and quick on the draw?
Can you jangle your spurs
and lay down the law?

Yep!

If you enter a classroom
and the cowboys are rowdy
can you obtain silence
just by hollerin' 'Howdy!'?

Yep!

Are you as at home in the saddle
as you are holding chalk?
Do you like eating baked beans?
Can you drawl when you talk?

Yep!

Can you herd cattle
and control a lasso?
If you answer *Yep!*
this job could be for you.

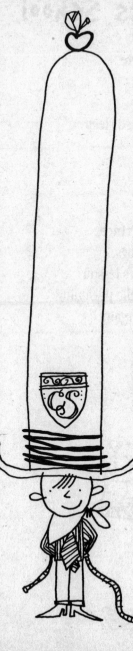

Yep!

But you gotta look good
in a ten-gallon hat
if you want to work here.
Any problem with that?

Nope!

Then mosey on down
for a tough interview
and show the posse
what you can do.

But one piece of advice
I'll give to you, son,
if they start shootin'
you better run.

It'll mean they don't like you.
They don't want you around.
You ain't been successful
so get outa town!

Bernard Young

Fairy-tale Princess School

Wednesday's Timetable

9.30 a.m. Christening Curses
This week: Methods of waking from enchanted sleep
without having to rely on a princely kiss.
(Several princesses have been disappointed
in the quality of prince thus obtained.)

10.30 a.m. How to recognize your Frog Prince
Princesses are forbidden to kiss the study frogs.
Princess Florabella kissed a frog in last week's lesson
and not only is she in hospital with salmonella poisoning
but got an extremely ugly prince into the bargain.

11 a.m. Break
Crowns are NOT to be worn in the playground.
Grudge the caretaker sustained a nasty flesh wound
when he sat on one which had been left on a bench.

11.15 a.m. Programming your mobile
An essential art if your father, the King,
stakes you out as bait for the local dragon.
A simple press of a button
will contact the knight in shining armour of your choice.

12 Midday Lunch
A light, but nutritious meal of thirty-four courses will be provided.
Do not speak to wicked enchanters outside the school gates
as the Princes' Union has called a strike
to protest about the practice of chopping princes' heads off
if they do not achieve tasks set by beautiful, but cruel princesses.
(these gels give princesses a bad name)
So there will be no one to rescue you
from the enchanters' towers till further notice.

2 p.m. Disguises
Today we are doing goosegirl, beggarmaid, kitchen skivvy and
    tattercoat,
all tried and tested by well-known princesses and
enabling even a novice to net a handsome prince.

2.30 p.m. Wicked stepmothers

Is your stepmother really an ogress? Has she a magic mirror?
Does she favour your two ugly stepsisters?
This is the first in a series of talks given by famous personalities.
Today, it's Snow White.
And remember, your highnesses, do not mention dwarves.
That business was all in the past.

3.30 p.m. Home-time

As paparazzi from various fairyland tabloids
have been pestering princesses as they clamber
into their golden carriages,
we have hired a wizard to blast them with his staff.
This should stop the nuisance
and highnesses are asked not to kick the resultant blackened bones
all over Grudge's clean courtyard.

Homework

We must ask princesses not to make their maids do it.
The maids are achieving better marks than their mistresses
and we all know what happens when maids get the upper hand.
They will impersonate you and marry your princes
and then where will you be?

Marian Swinger

Watch Carefully . . .

The teacher at the school for ghosts
Was really in full swing,
With ghostly drawings on the board,
And all that sort of thing.

She'd spent the lesson teaching them
Just how to walk through the walls –
She asked them, 'Do you understand?
We don't want any falls.'

A little ghostie raised his hand
And said with furrowed brow,
'Please, miss, I listened carefully
But still I'm not sure how.'

The teacher told him, 'That's OK,'
And reached out for her pen.
'Now all look closely at the board
And I'll go through it again . . .'

Clive Webster

Give Me Some Space

It's awful teaching kids in space
It really isn't nice.
They float around and bob about
And orbit round me twice.

Martian boys and girls are bright
And work out sums quite tricky
But their fingerprints are made of sludge
Which makes the pages sticky.

It's hard to keep the discipline
And show them who the boss is
When they'd rather play their favourite game –
Astronauts and crosses.

Julian Garfield

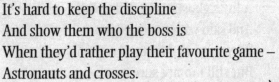

'Repeat After Me . . .'

At 'Déjà Vu' School
Work is *always* the same;
If they've done it *before*,
They just *do it again*!

Trevor Harvey

Snake Seminary

This is
a quiet school,
the loudest noise
a soft, soft hiss.

Here are
no desks or chairs;
the pupils coil their tails
and sit on them
as if at prayer.
They write their letters
with forked tongues
on the cool air.

They sit quite still,
attentive
and aware,
using their senses well.
In their smooth
sculptured heads
deep knowledge
slowly grows.

Their eyes stare
with such wisdom
with such power
that when they slither
out into the world
their looks stir
ancient memories,
strike fear.

Patricia Leighton

Correct Spelling

Witches spend no time at all
On TV or on comics.
They spend eight hours each day at school
On Witch Home Economics.

They learn the latest recipes
For most black-magic charms.
They know the best ingredients
To cause deep, dark alarms.

These witches stick to basics.
That truth I have to tell.
The modern witch, though trendy,
Knows so well how to spell!

John Kitching

SPECTACULARS SUPREME
Rome's Premier School for the Gladiatorial Arts

RULES FOR ALL GLADIATORS

- Swords and helmets always polished

- Muscles oiled and looking trim

- Girlfriends not allowed on fight days

- Orgies when results are in

- Enter with a macho swagger

- Snarl and wave your fist around

- If you're winning make it look good

- If you're losing spew and groan

- Keep it moving

- Keep it snappy

- Give the crowd a descent show

- If you're in a real humdinger play it to the Emperor's row

- When it's over shout 'Hail, Caesar!'

- Thank the gods you're still alive

- Easy on the 'I'm the greatest!'

- Do not wink at Caesar's wife

Break these rules and you'll be sorry,
Keep them and you might survive
Long enough to gain your freedom.
Roman pigs might also fly.

Patricia Leighton

School for Robots

Welcome to our
Ro-Bo School:
we're sure you're
not surprised to see
the first session,
of every day,
is just like yours,
'Assembly'.

Mike Johnson

The School for Spring

My first teaching job
was at the School for Spring

For years I worked there
teaching lambs to jump,
teaching buds how to open
and flowers to bloom.

Be careful tuition
I trained the sun
to get up a little earlier each day.

I taught the cold hard rain
to be gentler
and warmer.

Daffodils,
crocuses
and cherry blossom
were my star pupils.

In my classes
even hibernating hedgehogs
would wake;
swallows travel
thousands of miles
to be there;
rare natterjack toads
would gather
and sing.

Nice for the while;
but such froth and fun
is not the stuff
of a lifelong career.

My new job
pays much better
and my classes are more solemn,
now I'm working
as a tutor
for the College of Autumn.

David Bateman

Seven Sorts of Schools

Our schools for saving fossil fuels
Are simply far too cool schools

And schools for watching dangerous duels
Are all bloodthirsty ghouls' schools.

And schools for growing huge toadstools
Are damp as puddles-'n'-pools schools

And schools for making April fools
Are easily ridiculed schools

And schools for feeding pigs and mules
Are fill-their-troughs-with-gruel schools

And schools for discipline and rules
Are always strict and cruel schools

And schools for training molecules
Are our most minuscule schools.

Nick Toczek

Colosseum Comprehensive

They learn
subtraction of limbs, division of guts,
the practical geometry of sword stabs and cuts;

they study
the argument of thrust, science of net and spear,
the handicraft of killing, philosophy of force and fear;

on each public holiday the class exam arrives
and afterwards
the janitors
sweep up the fallen, waste of lives

Dave Calder

Arachnid Academy

In a dark cupboard, down under the stairs
There's a school full of spiders who're plying their wares.
They're learning fine arts to make themselves scary.
How to appear huge and make their legs hairy.
They're waiting and baiting, they're anticipating,
To capture, entrap you and slowly de-sap you!
They get marks out of ten for web-making skills
And points added on for the number of kills.
They don't take packed lunches, they catch what they eat.
Bluebottles, black beetles and greenflies complete!
They're taught to be frightening, scuttling like lightning,
So beware, they'll ensnare you and horribly scare you!
Their leader has shown them the tricks of the trade
To climb under pillows of beds left unmade!
To hide in dark corners until they are sure
That when they jump out, you can't head for the door.
They're lurking and loitering, they're lying in wait
to threaten, upset you and quietly torment you!

Diane Humphrey

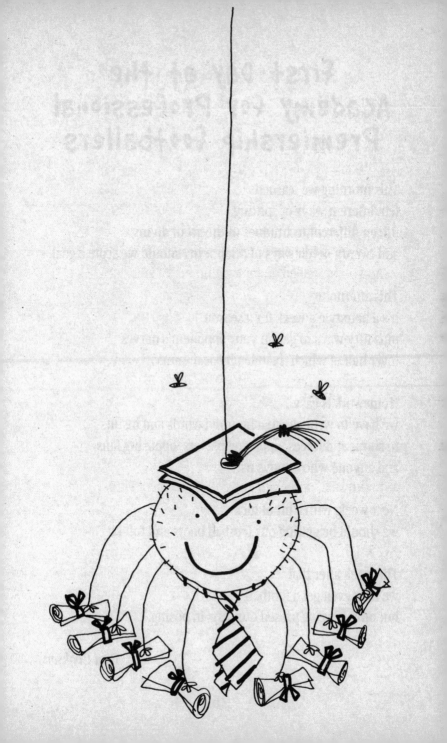

First Day at the Academy for Professional Premiership footballers

This morning we learned
ten different ways of spitting,
fifteen different techniques in the art of diving
and twenty-seven ways of celebrating should we score a goal.

This afternoon
it's a hairstyle a week for a season
plus fifty ways to get on your opponent's nerves
(over half of which include physical injury).

Homework is easy . . .
we have to write down a hundred words and insults
to shout at referees, opposing players, opposing fans
and anyone who annoys us.

Next week, with a bit of luck
we should be getting our football boots and full kit.

The week after that
we may even get a football
but only if we've passed our tests in posing.

Paul Cookson

The Very Brainy
Inventors School

Last week we were given our first toolkit
Crammed with everything we need
Just look at this lot;
    Twenty-two Twoddle-Tweezers
    Seventeen Blooper-Bungers
    Fourteen Fandangle-Irons
    Twelve Tworkle-Twisters (Left-hand thread)
    Twelve Tworkle Twisters (Right-hand thread)
    One Scrunch-Socket
    Five Fizzle-Pliers
    Seven Sproogle-Drivers
    A Dozen Dry-Dipstick-Drills
        Thirteen Thunder-Jumpers
        Twenty-One Woo-Wangle Wires
        A Short-Shanked Shuggle Shaver
        Six packets of assorted screws
        And three rubber bands.

5A

We were told to start inventing
Use our big brains, so we did
Here's what I've made so far;
    Electric cheese
    Bubble-gum-flavoured cabbage
    A little-brother-shutter-upper-kit
    A big-sister-teasing-set
    Glow-in-the-dark-underpants
    Everlasting fireworks (loud ones)
    An instant-recall-how-to-do-hard-sums-machine
    Clockwork fish and chips
    Mushroom-and-liver-flavoured custard
    A thermo-magnetic teacher shrinker
    An intergalactic pea-shooter
    Fizzy ballpoint-pen ink (orange flavoured)
    Indestructible footballs
    And a hand-held-homework gadget
    That always gets it right.

Next week I'll build a giant rocket
To rescue all you kids from school
Want to book a seat right now?

David Harmer

The High School for Haikus

seventeen of us in class,
writing poems in this style,
homework just three lines . . .

lessons don't last long
over before they begin,
seventeen minutes . . .

chips are counted out
so are carrots, beans at lunch,
total – seventeen . . .

football's not much fun,
first to seventeen will win,
if we have the time . . .

guess the leaving age
or the number of teachers,
obvious really . . .

I want to count less,
sometimes I want to count more,
sick of seventeen . . .

so even though I excelled
I want to get expelled
to give me the time
for developing rhyme
and kennings and sonnets and cinquains and raps
and limericks, couplets and blank verse as well.

Paul Cookson

(*A haiku is a Japanese poem of three lines, with
five syllables in the first line, seven syllables in
the second, and five again in the third line.*)

School for Haiku Writers

Japanese poet

Sits at the back of the class.

Has a small IQ.

Brian Patten

School Rules

Do wear a skateboard to breakfast.

Do dance on the new settee and use your bed as a trampoline.

Do perform handstands under the low-hanging light fitting.

Do ignore all rules about safety

Do jump on small visitors.

Do scare everyone with your extrovert behaviour

Do parachute from the tallest part of the building daily

Do come to school on a one-wheeled bicycle

Do expect high marks for getting into fights

Do expect letters of commendation home to parents if you are
    keen to perform any highly dangerous acts

Do make sure you are insured for personal damage

After all this is the school for stuntmen.

Margaret Blount

A Special School for the 'Boys in Blue'

The school that policemen go to
And go to school they do
Is found not far from Scotland Yard
On Letsby Avenue.

You learn to gather evidence
You learn to look for clues
You learn those special phrases
That all good bobbies use.

Book him! Cuff him!
'Ello, 'Ello, 'Ello
You're nicked old son
It's time to go.

You're trained to use your batons
Your cuffs and all that clobber
Then at break you can relax
By playing 'Cops and Robbers'.

You're issued with your size-ten boots
Whatever size your feet
And then you're taught that funny walk
You'll use when on the beat.

So all you budding cops now know
That there's a school for you
A special school for the 'Boys in Blue'
On Letsby Avenue.

Richard Caley

My Plastic Surgery Classes Are Just Not Going Well

My plastic surgery classes are just not going well
There's three spare ears over here like melted caramel
A nose that has four nostrils and still it cannot smell
No, my plastic surgery classes are just not going well

Someone else has seven eyes (to see them through the week)
Lashes on their forehead and eyebrows on their cheek
And after only minutes the face I lifted fell
No, my plastic surgery classes are just not going well

Tummy tucks have come unstuck and drag along the ground
The chest implants are far too large (at least they'll never drown)
I like to cover wrinkles with a splodge of *Polycell*
No, my plastic surgery classes are just not going well

Thanks to my foot pump most lips are looking fuller
Inflating like balloons, they've gone a funny colour
Floating off into the blue, watch them sway and swell
No, my plastic surgery classes are just not going well

To inject someone with *Botox* is the latest thing to do
And even though I cannot spell it's something I do too
But I injected someone's *buttocks* . . . you should have heard the yell
No, my plastic surgery classes are just not going well

Once my alteration operation is complete
I shouldn't leave the patients directly in the heat
That melts the sticky skin that slimes like sister's setting gel
No, my plastic surgery classes are just not going well

I got my motto wrong – one stitch in nine saves time
So now I've got a new job with a Doctor Frankenstein
He likes the fact they all look like turtles with no shell
So yes, my plastic surgery classes are progressing well!

Paul Cookson

The Dinner Lady Boot Camp School

D-I-N, D-I-N, D-I-DOUBLE-N, E-R!
D-I-N, D-I-N, D-I-DOUBLE-N, E-R!

We march and drill around the square
A grim and ghastly sight
We are your very worst nightmare
You'll never sleep at night
A rough and tough commando troop
We don't like kids at all
Your heads will sag and shoulders droop
Inside the dinner hall.

D-I-N, D-I-N, D-I-DOUBLE-N, E-R!
D-I-N, D-I-N, D-I-DOUBLE-N, E-R!

The dinner lady boot camp crews
Do not bring the best of news
Our training tells us how to use
Bulging muscles and tattoos
Flapping tabards, size-twelve shoes
We'll make you eat revolting stews
Sausages like doggy-doos
Vegetables of horrid hues
That stink like the inside of zoos

So do you need so many clues
To guess the happiness we choose?
Our anger has a shortened fuse
You'll leap like frightened kangaroos
Decide to hide inside the loos
We love your tears and loud boo-hoos
We always win and never lose
The dinner lady boot camp crews
The dinner lady boot camp crews.

D-I-N, D-I-N, D-I-DOUBLE-N, E-R!
D-I-N, D-I-N, D-I-DOUBLE-N, E-R!

We've trained for weeks and months and years
And now we've reached our prime
We'll soon have you in floods of tears
Every dinner time
When lunchtime comes we'll spoil your fun
You'll stand out in the rain
We'll shout and yell and get you done
Time and time again.

D-I-N, D-I-N, D-I-DOUBLE-N, E-R!
D-I-N, D-I-N, D-I-DOUBLE-N, E-R!

David Harmer

Welcome Speech at Saint Cholmondeley's School for Cheats

Welcome!
Welcome to Saint Cholmondeley's School for Cheats.
I am Mr Conningham, the Head Cheater.

Here at the Cholmondeley,
we are proud of our courses,
and we are sure that you will enjoy
our specialist courses in Cheating at Cards,
Team-Sports, and Indoor Games,
as well as our more ordinary courses
in Cheating at Maths, English,
Geography, History,
and two foreign languages.

Here at Cholmondeley's,
however, we are also strict.
Marks will be taken away
if you are caught not copying from the person next to you
(unless you have already sneaked a look at the answers beforehand,
in which case bonus points will be awarded).
Habitual non-skivers will be given detentions
at which they must fail to turn up without fail.

41

You will be expected to become experts
at slick excuses and forged letters;
and if you can find new ways
of pretending to do work
while not actually doing any,
then so much the better.

Later, you will have the exciting choice
between Cheating at Arts,
Cheating at Science,
And Cheating at Business –
but that is for the future.

Now Mrs Fraudulike will give you your house badges.
Oh. I see they have already been stolen.
That's something I like to see
– a new class that shows promise from the start.

Provided you play unfairly by us,
then we will play unfairly by you
– and I can't say fairer than that.

If you cheat hard at Cholmondeley's
during the years you are here,
I am sure that each and every one of you
will graduate (with First Class Dishonours)
when you leave,
ready to face an unsuspecting world
with an Ace
(or probably several Aces)
hidden up your sleeve.

David Bateman

Hell's Angel Class

We're a class of Hell's Angels.
We're awkward little tikes.
We never toil; drink engine oil,
And rev our motorbikes.

Our teacher tries to keep control.
We stop her all the time!
She shouts, 'Come here!' while we swig beer
And drink bottles of wine

No one likes to teach us!
Our filthy clothes, they stink!
We ride in class, say, 'Kiss my *#*!',
Do wheelies in the sink.

We cannot read, we cannot write
But we really do not care.
You have no fans, with
filthy hands,
Bad breath and
greasy hair.

Chris Ogden

Angel Class

We're a class of angels.
We always sit up straight.
Our hair is clean, we're never mean,
And we're seldom ever late!

Our work is neat and tidy,
Our writing's very good.
We raise our hand to understand
And find out what we should.

We always pay attention.
We never mess about.
We read our books, give pleasant looks,
And never scream and shout.

We're always doing goodly deeds
We try to help all creatures.
Our halos shine most of the time,
We value all our teachers!

Chris Ogden

46

An Alien's First Week at Earth School

today we've got hisstory
the story of hissing
then we've got fizzicks
the science of fizzing
later is jography
the way to go jogging
then we have mew-sick
about illness of moggies
tomorrow more sighence
the study of sighing
my favourite's buyology
the science of buying
then there is 'eart
about beating and being
and finally PE
the time to be –
keeping your mouth shut

Trevor Millum

SHOOTING STARS:
End of Term Examination

YOU HAVE TWO HOURS. ANSWER THREE QUESTIONS

1. What is the maximum number of wishes you can grant, at any one time and why is there a limit?

2. What should you do, if you know a wish is harmful to others, probably going to do wrong or is of bad intention?

3. When should you grant wishes, but not quite in the way intended?

4. What should you do if someone wishes for herds of unicorns, gardens full of jewel-studded peacocks, a phoenix?

5. What should you do if someone wishes for a mile-high ice cream, lakes of chocolate, Concorde-sized Christmas cake?

6. What is the importance of chasing rainbows, looking on the bright side, finding silver linings in even the darkest cloud?

7. How can you most quickly turn tears to smiles, fear to friendship, loathing to laughter?

Mike Johnson

LEAD BALLOON
SKY DIVING SCHOOL

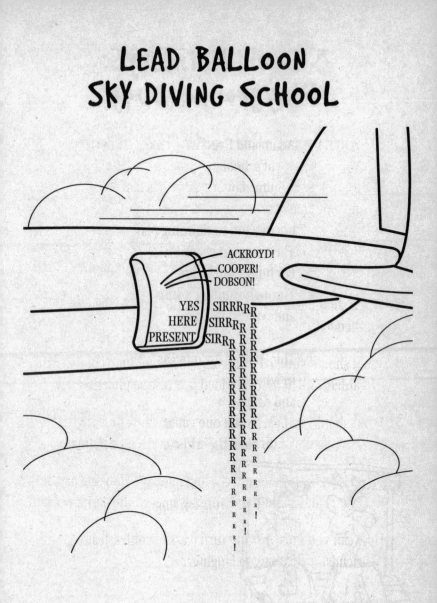

Tony Langham

Eden Primary
Playground Duty

Adam and Eve
    at school
    one day

hurried out to morning play
They ran and chased
For hours and hours
Through summer's suns
and winter showers.

They played for months
in wind
and drizzle
    . . . as no one came
    to blow the whistle.

Peter Dixon

Vacuum Cleaners' Misdemeanours

Young vacs play games:
call teachers names
like '*suckers*' or '*old bags*';

they muck about
when on the scout
for dust and ash and fags

by blowing out –
on purpose flout
the simplest diagrams

and sure enough
they always fluff
their end-of-term exams.

Gina Douthwaite

Just Joking

If you want a career in practical joking,
there's a school with an ideal format:
as you walk through the door you get a good soaking
from a sprinkler disguised as a doormat.
The whole of the hall has a terrible pong,
the teachers are wacky and weird –
they throw custard pies if you get something wrong,
and the headmistress wears a false beard.

The maths books are written in Greek and Chinese,
with diagrams drawn upside down;
the playground's a bog where you sink to your knees
in mud of indelible brown.
There are big plastic spiders all over the floor
that jump up with a frightening whoosh;
the school bus is programmed for breakdowns galore,
so you all have to get out and push.

The library's stocked with books where the words
all fade before you can read them;
the biology lab is full of stuffed birds
which change colour whenever you feed them.
The computers explode at the press of a switch
and cover the pupils with flour
with a secret ingredient that gives you an itch
and bursts into flames in the shower.
The school clocks run backwards from night until morning
and chime with a kind of a cough;
the fire alarm sounds twice an hour without warning,
and the cloakroom has hooks that fall off.
The chairs make a noise like a fart when you sit,
and your desk will collapse when you write on it;
the school meals have gravy that looks just like spit
and glows green if you shine a bright light on it.

In this hotbed of horror the days all seem long,
and you'll finish up twisted but clever;
so – all join together to sing the school song –
practical jokers for ever!

John Irwin

Snail School Pupil

I'm an asymmetrical mollusc, or what you would call a snail.
I'm a pupil at the Gastropod School, and I'm afraid I'll fail
At the end-of-term exams, because I'm not much good at Slime.
Mine only comes in fits and starts, not in a long straight line.
At Speedy Shell Retraction I'm the fastest in my class,
Also Holding Still Inside the Shell until the dangers pass.

How to
avoid
birds

Antennae Raise and Scanning is a bit more hard to do
Cos you have to decode messages and act upon them too.
But I know the danger signals, like when blackbirds are around,
For they pick up unsuspecting snails and bash them on the ground.
The thing to do if one flies down is shoot into your shell
And sit in fear and trembling and feeling quite unwell.

Preventing Flight's more difficult, for birds might, for their pleasure,
Just pick you up and fly away to eat you at their leisure.
And then there's pesky gardeners who fling their snails next
  door –
Or stamp their boot-heels on your shell and squash you to the floor
So your shell goes scrunch and all the rest of you goes squelch
  and splats!

– So I'd better start revising or I'll never pass my SATs!

Pam Gidney

Princess School

I'm going to Princess School next summer term.
I've got my uniform, a floor-length satin number
with emerald green sash and a dainty diamond
tiara, my mother paid cash.

I'm going to Princess School next summer term,
where we write in brand-new notebooks every day
and children arrive by helicopter
and there's an Olympic stadium for afternoon play.

I'm going to Princess School next summer term,
where we have a morning nap to catch
up on our dreams and our school dinners are served
on silver platters, we have Caviar and Ice cream.

I'm going to Princess School next summer term,
where we're taught in classes of One.
I'll sit on my own throne and send paper
Lear Jets out of the windows for fun.

I'm going to Princess School next summer term,
my new teacher is Miss Golden Hair, her shouting
voice has been surgically removed and she's not
allowed to swear.

I'm going to Princess School next summer term,
to mix with all the toffs: with Beatrice, Tamara,
Angelina, I'm sure they'll all be boffs.

If there's a question I don't know, I'll keep
    quiet
and smile and get the answer from my new
    best friend –
a top of the range Internet mobile.

Roz Goddard

School Rules for Young Snowmen

Don't laugh
Don't talk
Don't fidget
Don't walk
Don't eat
Don't drink
Don't hiccup
Don't blink
Don't sleep
Don't snore
Don't fall on the floor
Don't dance
Don't sing
Don't do anything
And most of all
Don't come in the hall
to warm up your toes
or your ears or nose
for everyone knows

RULE 1
Stay out
of the sun

that if you unfroze . . .

then . . .

we'd have to start you all over again.

Kate Williams

Dragon School Song

Saint George rode out a-questing
In a knightly sort of way,
Seeking Maidens he could rescue,
Seeking Dragons he could slay,
But the Dragons when he challenged them
Could only say:

We doan wanna eat the Lady
We doan wanna fight the Knight
All that smoking makes yer choke 'n
Sets yer teeth alight.
Nuthin's worse 'n eatin person
An' we doan think fightin's right.

We doan wanna fry yer granny,
Or bar-B-Q yer mum.
We doan wanna growl 'r yowl 'r howl
FEE-FI-FO-FUM!
We are People-Friendly Dragons.
Will yer be our chum?

If yer come roun fer the weekend
We c'n do the things yer like:
You c'n bat when we play cricket,
We c'n mend yer bike,
But the teeniest hint of fightin'
An' we go on strike.

We c'n dance a tarantella
We c'n make a daisy chain,
We c'n shimmy in the sunshine,
We c'n rumba in the rain,
Any fun thing, but fer one thing
An' that's VERY plain.

We doan wanna eat the Lady
We doan wanna fight the Knight
All that smoking makes yer choke 'n
Sets yer teeth alight.
Nuthin's worse 'n eatin person
An' we doan think fightin's right.

John Whitworth

The class(ified) register at St Incognito's School for Spies

Master of disguise:
Smith, A.

For the period XX/XX/XXXX to XX/XX/XXXX

Pupil	M	T	W	T	F			M	T	W	T	F
1 Smith, A.	✔	✔	✔	✔	✔		Smith, A.	✔	✔	✔	✔	✔
2 Smith, A.	✔	✔	✔	✔	✔		Smith, A.	✔	✔	✔	✔	✔
3 Smith, A.	✔	✔	✔	✔	✔		Smith, A.	✔	✔	✔	✔	✔

Philip Waddell

Stone Age School

In stone age days
In stone age schools
      (stone age teachers
      stone age rules),
it must have been a stone age larf
      in maths or science
      or art and craft
to see the teachers standing there
in only bits of skin and hair!

and just imagine what a sight
the school would be on parents' night
      as mums and dads
      in pelts of creatures
stood in queues to see the teachers
      mammoth pants
      shirts that tickle
      itchy vests and bras of bristle.

My mum, your mum, dads galore
posy parents by the score . . .
      stone age days
stone age tables
stone age clothes
      Designer labels

Peter Dixon

The School for Daydreamers

Lesson One

Gaze out
of the window.
Let your mind wander. Do
not listen to a word I say.
Begin . . .

I rang
a bell. I beat
a drum. No one stirred. No
one heard. Your thoughts were far away.
Well done.

Homework

Drift off
during your tea.
Don't watch TV. Tune in
to the pictures inside your head.
Have fun.

Bernard Young

Fishy Tales

Monsters: blue, humpbacked, bottle-nosed,
learn to swim in secret classrooms
how to gorge on krill and plankton
breathe through blowholes making fountains
on the surface of the sea.

Nose-dive deep for flipping lessons
scrutinize the sea by listening
tell their scary tales by crooning
spooky spellbound echoed sounds
that resound for miles around.

Sounds like they're having
a whale of a time.

Lynne Taylor

'Gnaw – Seah'

'Gnaw – Seah' [College for School Cooks]
Principal: Miss B. Queasy.
School Rules.

Mashed potato must always have lumps
And gravy glisten with grease.
Cabbages, cauliflowers, peas as well,
Like sweaty feet should strongly smell.

Semolina slop should be grey and thick,
No disgrace if it makes you sick.
Jamless doughnuts always should
Be rock hard when served as pud.

Get the kids in queues to wait,
Hurl the food on every plate.
Scowl and mutter before they sit,
'Don't dare leave a single bit!'

Always note these golden rules
When you get in one of our schools.
Then you'll be – without question,
In total charge of indigestion.

Redvers Brandling

Slack Street School

So this is the school
Unlike the rest
That punishes those
Who do their best
And praises those
Who do their worst
Cos everything here
Has been reversed.

All shoes must be muddy.
We have to chew chuddy
And not close the school gate
But stroll into school late
And drop lots of litter
And chatter and twitter
And flick things and take things
And kick things and break things,
And practise our yawning
For most of the morning

Cos this is the school
Unlike the rest
That punishes those
Who do their best
And praises those
Who do their worst
Cos everything here
Has been reversed.

Our schoolbags get hidden
And maths is forbidden
So's writing and reading,
Though we're all succeeding
At learning misspelling,
Nail-biting, tale-telling,
Bad manners and crudeness.
We've lessons in rudeness
And swinging on coat hooks
And doodling in notebooks

Cos this is the school
Unlike the rest
That punishes those
Who do their best
And praises those
Who do their worst
Cos everything here
Has been reversed.

We copy and cheat and
Fill walls with graffiti.
We're taught to be vandals,
To cause minor scandals
On which they assess us,
Then gov'nors address us
And sack all the sad brats
Who've done well in their SATs.
Deliberate excelling
Means instant expelling

Cos this is the school
Unlike the rest
That punishes those
Who do their best
And praises those
Who do their worst
Cos everything here
Has been reversed.

Nick Toczek

School for Nice Children who are Always Top of the Class

Nine o'clock
How to whisper, cough, giggle
And drop marbles in assembly

Nine-twenty
How to race along corridor

Nine-twenty-five
Maths – how to muddle up number blocks
And forget five-times table

Ten o'clock
English – how to forget capital letters
And full stops

Ten-forty-five
How to drop litter in playground
And kick ball on to roof

Eleven o'clock
How to talk in line
And answer teacher back

One minute past eleven
How to fidget
Outside Head's office

Two minutes past eleven
How to be sullen and rude

Three minutes past eleven
How to stand in school entrance
Waiting for Mum
Who has been called away from work

How to have regrets

Roger Stevens

A Letter from the Head of the Zombie Academy

Motto: A stitch in time saves nine

Dear Parents

I crave your attention, nay, beg,
for here in lost property, we have a leg,
a selection of arms and a box full of toes
as well as six hands and a rather large nose.
There's a jar crammed with eyeballs,
three ears and a tongue,
an unmentionable organ
and an old pair of lungs
plus forty-six brains
(which just goes to show
why this school's exam marks
are always so low).
But to come to the point,
I must ask, nay, I beg
that the owners of all
these odd parts and this leg
collect them at once
for they've been here too long
and the lost property cupboard
is starting to pong.

Or we'll just have to sell them
on bring-and-buy day
to the Frankenstein School
(just a shuffle away)
with proceeds to RTD
(Raising The Dead).
Best wishes, dear parents
from your own
                Zombie Head.

Marian Swinger

Invisibility School

Roger Stevens

Time Travellers College: Seven Messages from the Form Teacher

Lastly, if you have forgotten anything I have said,
Go back three minutes to hear these notices again.
Sixthly, I have the results of tomorrow's history test
And I will be very pleased with the results.
Fifthly, the school's centenary was exactly five years ago
And I expect to see all of you lot there.
Fourthly, the under-fourteens football team drew 0–0
In their cup game tomorrow
But they won the replay last week.
Thirdly, I understand that many students from this class
Have already been to the end-of-term Christmas party.
You are all reminded that you are only allowed one mince pie
And that the head will be checking the dining room in the future.
Secondly, there have been reports of students arriving late to
    lessons.
Those who do will have to catch up work in their own time.
Firstly, there will be a fire drill yesterday.

John Coldwell

The School of Contortionists

The School of Contortionists
The Long and Winding Road

Dear Mr and Mrs Foldaway,

Your son has fitted in well at school
Being ready to bend over backwards
In order to help others.

He is top of the class at tying himself in knots
And has managed to get his knickers
and most parts of his body in a twist.

There are some subjects in which he needs to be stretched
And, he must remember that *every* time he opens his mouth
He must put his foot in it.

Yours truly

Mr Twistanturner
(The Head – Shoulders, Knees and Toes, Knees and Toes)

PS
We have organized a school trip to the circus
If you would like your son to go,
I am sure we could squeeze him in.

John Coldwell

Chicken School

Period one – simple clucking
Period two – more clucking
Period three – clucking with attitude
Period four – clucking with indecision
Period five – pecking in dirt
Period six – pecking in gravel
Period seven – rhythmic and jerky neck movements
Period eight – clucking (revision)

Roger Stevens

Jester's School

I've found the perfect school for me
It's called the Jester's School
The teachers there encourage you
To simply act the fool.

Richard Caley

Coldheart Towers Student Prospectus

Email:Vena@Coldheartblood.com

COLDHEART TOWERS is the foremost school for Nosferatu
Headmistress: Dr Vena Cava V.A. (Hons) Transylvania. M. Ed.

Curriculum includes
- ✔ Architecture
- ✔ Bewitching
- ✔ Deception
- ✔ Transformation
- ✔ Bloodology
- ✔ Nosferatu History
- ✔ Gothic Literature
- ✔ Flying
- ✔ Coffin design
- ✔ Viledin lessons by arrangement

Uniform
Boys: White frill shirts, black trousers, shoes, socks and cape.
Girls: Long purple dress, red shoes, black stockings and cape.

All students will need:

Crypts, Coffins and Candles by Esmeralda Raven
Is the Sun a Myth? by Richard Richvayne
Velvet Echoes: A Critical Guide to Costume by Roski Rouge
The Oxford Compendium of Tombstones, Effigies and Epitaphs
Whispering Wraiths: a Dictionary of Ghouls and Phantoms
How to Bewitch and Befuddle by Scarlett McGhoul
Defeating Slayers and Other Enemies by M. Taint
Literature:
Macbeth by William Shakespeare
Poetry of Edgar Allan Poe
Dracula by Bram Stoker

Students must provide own coffins for sleeping. (No stone)

Non Jugulum Jugulare

Angela Topping

Higher Education

My school is one that trembles
my school is one that shakes
my school is one that's nervous
my school is one that quakes.

My school is one that rumbles
and quivers, gargles, growls,
it sounds as if an illness
is troubling its bowels.

Inspectors never visit
and parents are too scared.
Beneath the floorboards belching,
that's huge, is often heard.

My school is really somewhere
that's way outside the norm . . .
. . . on top of a volcano . . .
. . . at least it's always warm.

Stewart Henderson

A Treasured Pupil

Ahoy there, Mrs Silver!
Young Johnny's going great.
He's a marvel with his cutlass
And his eye patch looks first-rate.
He always does his homework
And always reads his book,
He varnishes his wooden leg
And polishes his hook.
There's only one small problem
That I can find with him –
If he wants to be a pirate
Then he'll have to learn to swim.

Julian Garfield

A selected list of titles available from Macmillan Children's Books

The prices shown below are correct at the time of going to press. However, Macmillan Publishers reserves the right to show new retail prices on covers which may differ from those previously advertised.

These titles are available at all good bookshops, can be ordered from our website, www.panmacmillan.com, and are also available by post from:

Bookpost
PO Box 29, Douglas, Isle of Man IM99 1BQ

Credit cards accepted. For details:
Telephone 01624 836000
Fax: 01624 670923
Email: bookshop@enterprise.net
www.bookpost.co.uk

Free postage and packing in the UK